The Little Bunny Rabbit

Jessica Hill

Scripture taken from the New King James Version.
Copyright © 1979, 1980, 1982 by Thomas Nelson, Inc. Used by permission. All rights reserved.

Archway Publishing books may be ordered through booksellers or by contacting:

Archway Publishing
1663 Liberty Drive
Bloomington, IN 47403
www.archwaypublishing.com
1 (888) 242-5904

Illustrations by: Shawn Horne

ISBN: 978-1-4808-2729-5 (sc)
ISBN: 978-1-4808-2728-8 (e)

Print information available on the last page.

Archway Publishing rev. date: 01/29/2016

There was a little bunny rabbit hopping down a very long and winding trail.

Along this trail he ran into different types of weather like rain and thunderstorms with lightning.

Snow and ice.

Darkness and sunshine.

Kind of like real life! He did get afraid from time to time but instead of giving up he kept going. He was told if he stayed on this path there would be a garden full of carrots at the end.

And boy oh boy was he HUNGRY!

If you were the rabbit what would you do when you were lonely or afraid? If we have Jesus in our hearts, we would talk to him and lean on him right?

One day as he was hopping
along the trail a little spider
jumped out and blocked it!

He put his front two legs up
and yelled out "HALT!"

Little bunny rabbit just where are you are going?" The bunny replied, "I'm going to the biggest garden full of carrots ever!" "Well sir", said the spider. "In all my 87 years I've never heard of that! Are you sure you were told correctly?" The little rabbit swallowed hard and replied, "yeah um well I guess so. I was told if I stay on this trail it will lead me there." "Ha!" said the spider. "How long have you been traveling it?" Bunny replied, "a little over 10 years." The spider instantly started laughing!!!

"What in the world? That's WAY TOO LONG! How have you managed to stay alive this long?" "Well sir", said the bunny. "God has protected me this far and I know as long as I keep him close to my heart he will always protect me. You see, all he asks is for us to love, obey, and believe in him and he promises we will live forever! Eternal life!"

"Well that sounds like a bunch of bologna to me", said the spider. "Live forever? Eternal life? What? Besides, who in their right mind would want to live forever anyway? I hate to break it to you but whoever told you that is just pulling your leg!"

"Pulling my legs?" said
the little rabbit with a
puzzled look on his face.

"Why would God do that? You know, God would never leave me or forsake me. You are the one that is pulling my leg. The problem is you don't have any faith but, you need to find it before it's too late. I would really hate to see you left behind and all alone."

So with that being said the little bunny rabbit just kept hopping down the trail. With no idea of what was in store for him or when he would reach the end. He just kept going with his heart full of faith.

Always remember to have faith. Trust and believe in GOD and all things will come! Matthew 21:22 We all have a garden of carrots waiting on us so stay hungry!!!!!!!

Ephesians 2:8-9 For by grace you have been saved through faith, and that not of yourselves; it is the gift of God, not of works, lest anyone should boast.

"This book is dedicated to my grandmother. Without the Godly influence you instilled in me I would be lost in this world. It would take an eternity to give back an ounce of what you have done for me. You are and have always been my idol! For my mother I want to thank you for the first time in my life for being there to "whip" me back in line! Without you I wouldn't be alive. You believed in me and pushed me many times WAY past my breaking point and you created the person that I am today. Mama you are and always have been my true HERO! My whole world changed when God blessed me with two intelligent, loving, hardworking, and kindhearted children. My whole life has been turned upside down, sideways, and everything in between and I wouldn't have it any other way. God saved me by giving me you and always know that as long as I live I will be there for you in every way possible. However, it doesn't stop there I met a man that is now my husband that just so happens to be the man of my dreams! You are an intellectual man with a beautiful bubbly personality. Thank you from the bottom of my heart for loving us, I am truly the luckiest woman in the world just to be able to call you mine! As for my stepdaughter you are strong and have potential that is off the charts. Most people your age could only dream of having the drive that you have within you! Special thanks to the Hill, Bailey, Morgan, Baltimore Church Family, and SPS family. Each and every one of you have been a powerful impact on my life!"

Jessica Hill has been passionate about writing since she was thirteen years old. She enjoys writing poetry, songs, and short stories. Church and learning about God and faith have always been strong priorities in her life. A wife and mother, she is also a youth leader at her church.

Printed in the United States
by Baker & Taylor Publisher Services